73009

£9.50

How Do We Taste and Smell?

Carol Ballard

WAYLAND

How Our Bodies Work

How Do Our Eyes See?

How Do Our Ears Hear?

How Do We Taste and Smell?

How Do We Feel and Touch?

How Do We Think?

How Do We Move?

Editor: Ruth Raudsepp
Illustrators: Kevin Jones Associates and Michael Courtney
Designer: Phil Jackson

First published in 1997 by Wayland Publishers Ltd, 61 Western Road,
Hove, East Sussex, BN3 1JD, England.

Find Wayland on the internet at http://www.wayland.co.uk

British Library Cataloguing in Publication Data
Ballard, Carol
How Do We Taste and Smell? – (How Our Bodies Work)
1. Taste - Juvenile literature 2. Smell - Juvenile literature
I. Title II. Jones, K. III. Courtney, M.

ISBN 0 7502 2068 6

Picture acknowledgements
The author and publishers thank the following for use of their photographs:
Cephas 5, 10; Chapel Studios *title page*, 15; Bruce Coleman 27(top);
Eye Ubiquitous 10; Chris Fairclough *cover*, 7, 12, 20, 22; Houses & Interiors 21;
Tizzie Knowles 25(top); Zul Mukhida 29; Science Photo Library 17;
Tony Stone 25(bottom); Zefa 4, 18, 27(bottom).
The remaining pictures are from the Wayland Picture Library.

Typeset by Phil Jackson
Printed in Italy by G Canale & C. S. p. A.

Contents

Taste and Smell

Everybody has tastes and smells they like and dislike. Some people love the taste of bananas while others do not like bananas at all. Some people like the smell of freshly roasted coffee beans while others do not.

Many foods have chemicals added to make them taste better. Medicines often have flavours added to hide a bitter taste and make them easier to swallow.

◀ We experience a wide variety of tastes and smells in the food we eat every day.

Our senses of taste and smell can warn us about the food we eat. Some food may look perfectly all right, but it may taste or smell bad.

▲
Milk which has been kept too long has a sharp smell and sour taste.

Our sense of smell can warn us about danger. We may smell gas, alerting us to a gas leak or smoke, alerting us about a fire.

This book will tell you about your senses of taste and smell and how they work.

Some cheeses, ▶ onions, garlic and spices have strong tastes and smells.

Inside the Mouth

The first parts of your mouth that food comes into contact with are your teeth. Sharp front teeth bite and tear off a piece of food. Your lower and upper jaw is hinged so it can move up and down and from side to side. As your jaw moves, food is crushed and ground between strong, flat teeth at the back of your mouth called molars.

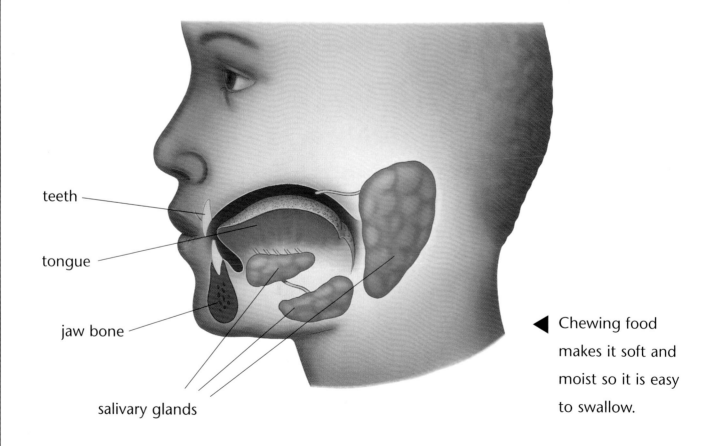

teeth

tongue

jaw bone

salivary glands

◀ Chewing food makes it soft and moist so it is easy to swallow.

As food is chewed it mixes with a watery liquid in the mouth called saliva. Saliva is made in **salivary glands** under the tongue and at the back of the mouth. Saliva makes the food soft and slippery.

Can you roll your tongue like this? The ability to roll your tongue often runs in the family.

The tongue moves food around the mouth. It has several muscles which allow it to move in any direction. As we chew, food slides over the rough, bumpy surface of the tongue and the taste of the food is detected.

Can you see the bumpy surface of your tongue? Curl your tongue and look at the underneath surface. Does it look smoother than the top surface? ▶

How Do Taste Buds Work?

Between the bumps on the surface of the tongue are groups of **cells** called taste buds. Taste buds detect the taste of food. Most people have about ten thousand taste buds on their tongue.

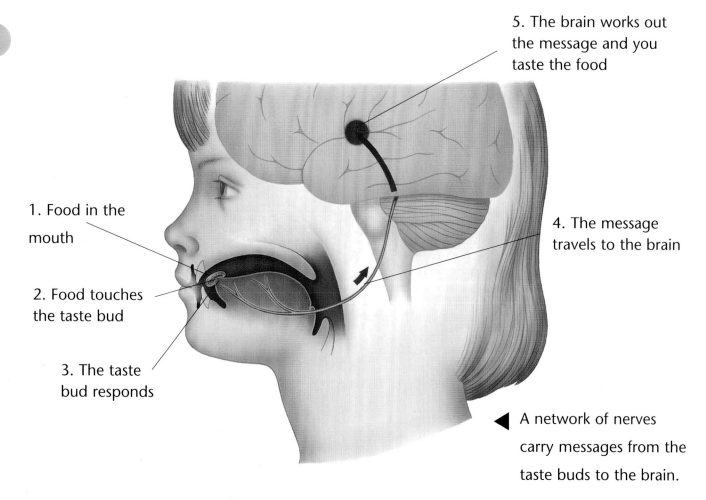

5. The brain works out the message and you taste the food

1. Food in the mouth

2. Food touches the taste bud

3. The taste bud responds

4. The message travels to the brain

◄ A network of nerves carry messages from the taste buds to the brain.

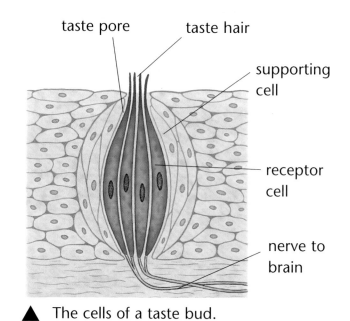

taste pore   taste hair

supporting cell

receptor cell

nerve to brain

▲ The cells of a taste bud.

The cells of a taste bud are rather like the segments of an orange. There are two types of cell in each taste bud: receptor cells, which detect the taste of the food, and supporting cells, which keep the taste bud together and give it its shape.

As food moves across the tongue, it touches tiny hairs on the receptor cells and enters the taste **pore**. The taste buds then send a message to the brain. The brain collects all the messages together and works out what the food tastes like.

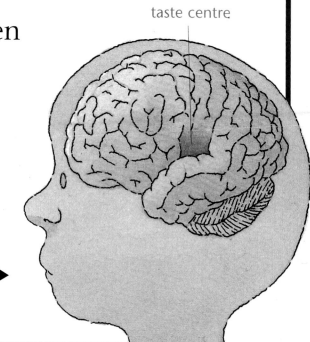

taste centre

Messages from the taste buds travel to the ▶ taste centre in the middle of the brain.

9

Sweet, Sour, Bitter and Salty

There are four basic tastes: sweet, sour, bitter and salty. The many tastes we make out are made up of different combinations of these four tastes.

Taste buds which respond to a sweet, sour, bitter and salty taste are clustered together on different parts of the tongue.

▲
Adding sugar to foods which contain acid can take away the sharp, sour taste.

◄ Many of our foods contain a mixture of different tastes.

◄ This girl is adding sweeteners to her coffee to make it taste less bitter.

Sweet tastes are detected on the tip of the tongue. Salty tastes are detected along each side of the tongue. The middle of each side of the tongue detects sour tastes and the back detects bitter tastes.

bitter

sour

sweet

salty

11

salty

▲

Areas on the tongue where we taste different flavours.

Foods such as jam and biscuits contain sugar or **artificial** sweeteners. Acids in foods make them taste sour. Oranges and lemons contain citric acid. Vinegar contains acetic acid. Coffee has a bitter taste. Some foods naturally contain salt. Others, such as potato crisps and salted peanuts, have salt added. Many people sprinkle extra salt onto their food.

Detecting Different Tastes

Try this test with a friend to see which parts of the tongue make out different tastes.

You will need three drinking straws and cups, two spoons, sugar, lemon juice, salt and water. Dissolve four teaspoons of sugar in half a cup of water. Put lemon juice into the next cup. Put one teaspoonful of salt into half a cup of water and stir until it dissolves.

◀ These children are trying to find out which parts of their tongues make out different tastes.

Always ask an adult before you put anything into your mouth!

Without telling your friend which solution you are using, suck up a drop with the straw. Put a drop on to the tip of your friend's tongue. If they can recognize the taste, record the result. If they cannot recognize the taste, put a drop of the same solution on a different part of their tongue. Keep doing this until they can recognize the taste. Record where on their tongue they detected the taste. When you have each tested the three solutions look at the results.

13

Solution Name	Sugar	Lemon	Salt
Me	X / X (X ✔)		
David			

▲ You could use a chart like this to record your results. Use a ✔ for a correct answer and a ✗ for a wrong answer.

Inside the Nose

Every time we breathe in, air is sucked through the nose, down the **windpipe** and into the lungs. When we breathe out, air is pushed out of the lungs, up the windpipe and out through the nose.

The bendy tip of the nose is made from a stiff substance called **cartilage**. Cartilage also separates the end of the nose into two nostrils.

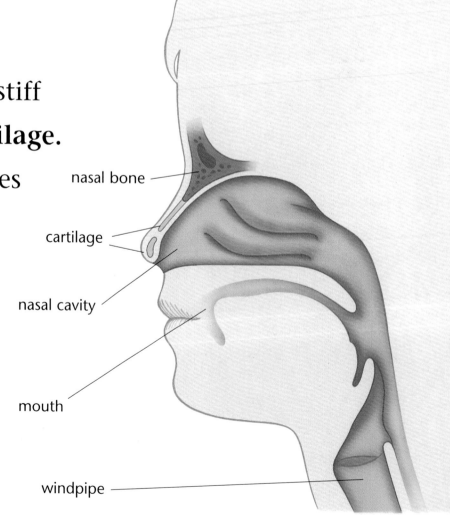

nasal bone

cartilage

nasal cavity

mouth

windpipe

The nasal cavity is linked to ▶ the mouth and the windpipe.

Behind the nostrils is the **nasal cavity**. This links the nostrils and the windpipe. The nasal cavity has a lining which does two jobs. It warms and moistens the air we breathe in and detects smells.

▲
Sniffing helps us to detect smells by 'pulling' more air into the nose.

Our sense of smell is much more sensitive than our sense of taste. Adults can usually detect about ten thousand smells. After being in a room with a smell for a while, we stop noticing it. But if a person enters the room they would notice the smell straight away.

Some flowers, like these daffodils, ▶ have a strong smell.

How We Smell

The lining at the top of the nasal cavity contains three types of cell which are involved in detecting smells.

The receptor cells in the lining of the nasal cavity detect smells. We have about twenty-five million receptor cells. Each receptor cell is long and thin, with tiny hairs at one end. Receptor cells live for about thirty days. They are continually replaced by basal cells which grow into new receptor cells. Supporting cells lie between the receptor cells and help to support them.

A hunting dog has about two hundred and twenty million receptor cells. Its sense of smell is ten times more sensitive than a human's.

As we breathe in, air passes over the receptor cells. Chemicals in the air dissolve in the watery layer on the inside of the nasal cavity. The hairs of the receptor cells detect these chemicals and the receptor cells send messages to the brain. The brain then works out the smell.

▲ These tiny hairs inside the nose act as a filter, stopping dust and dirt entering the nasal cavity.

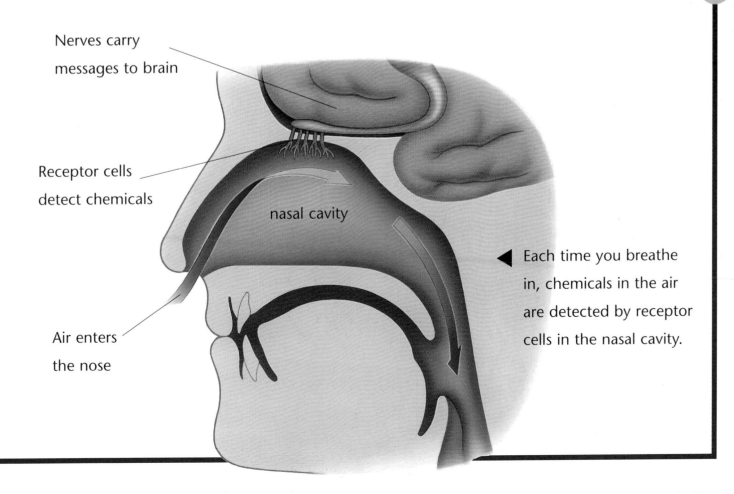

Nerves carry messages to brain

Receptor cells detect chemicals

nasal cavity

Air enters the nose

◀ Each time you breathe in, chemicals in the air are detected by receptor cells in the nasal cavity.

A Blocked Nose

The most common cause of a blocked nose is a cold, caused by a **virus.** The lining of the nasal cavity swells and extra fluid collects. It is hard for air to pass through the fluid so we tend to breathe through our mouth instead of through our nose. This means that only a little air passes the receptor cells in the nasal cavity, so our sense of smell is reduced.

◀ When our nose is blocked we cannot smell properly.

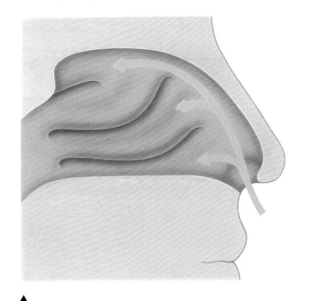

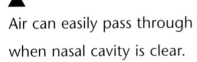

Air can easily pass through when nasal cavity is clear.

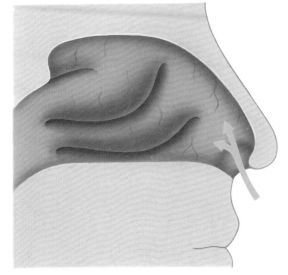

▲

Air cannot pass through when the nasal cavity is blocked with fluid.

Allergies can cause the same effects as a cold. People who are allergic to something try to avoid coming into contact with it. For example, hay fever sufferers stay indoors when there is a lot of grass pollen in the air. If they do not, their bodies react to the grass pollen and their nasal cavities become blocked with fluid.

Because there is no **gravity** in space, fluids can collect ▶ in the head. Astronauts often feel as if they have a cold and a blocked nose.

Taste and Smell Work Together

We can tell the difference between many different flavours. Some of these differences are very obvious, for example, few people would confuse the flavour of cabbage with chocolate!

▲
Too much or too little salt can spoil our enjoyment of food or drink.

◀ If we had to rely only on taste or on smell we would not be able to taste as many flavours as we can using both senses.

Some people can make out very slight differences in taste and smell. Skilled wine tasters can recognize the type of grape from which a wine is made, the country and even the vineyard where the grapes were grown.

There are many types of smell. The brain puts together messages from the taste buds and nasal cavity, allowing us to make out many flavours.

A chef uses his senses of taste and smell, by adding a pinch of herbs to improve the flavour of the food. ▶

Taste Activity

Try this test with a friend to find out whether you really do need to smell your food in order to work out its taste.

Cut up banana, carrot, apple, melon, chocolate, cheese and bread into cubes. You need two cubes of each type of food for each person who is going to be tested.

22

◀ These children are trying to find out whether their sense of smell helps them to detect the flavour of food.

Ask an adult to help you when cutting up food.

Cover your friend's eyes. Then tell them to pinch their nostrils together. Put one cube of food on to their tongue and let them chew it.

Record what they think it is in the results table (shown below). Do the same with each type of food in turn. (If you have some very strong flavours, the person being tested may need a mouthful of water in between each food.)

23

Repeat the test, but this time without your friend holding their nose. What do the results tell you? Does a sense of smell help identify the flavours of food?

	Me		David		Dad	
	B	U	B	U	B	U
Banana	✗	✔	✗	✔	✔	✔
Carrot	✗	✔	✗	✔		
Melon	✔	✔				
Apple						
Chocolate						
Cheese						

B = blocked nose   U = unblocked nose

▲ Record your results on a table like this.

Artificial Tastes and Smells

Think about the taste and smell of an orange. You know that the juice will have a sharp, tangy taste and that the smell will linger on your fingers for a while.

▲
Will the juice from the fresh orange taste like that from the carton? Which do you think will taste better?

Does orange juice from a carton taste the same? Not usually, because extra things are added to the pure orange juice. Ingredients, such as sugar, are added to change or improve the flavour. Other chemicals are added to improve its colour and keep it fresh for longer.

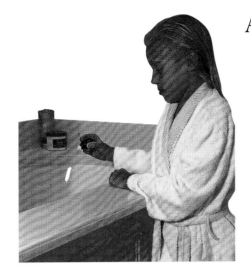

An ancient form of medicine called aromatherapy uses highly-perfumed oils from plants to treat many illnesses and aches and pains. People may rub the scented oils into their skin, add a few drops to their bath or make up a strong-smelling liquid and breathe in the vapour.

▲
This girl is adding lavender oil to her bath water for a relaxing bath.

Aromatherapists use many different plant oils and rub them into the skin to treat illnesses and relieve stress.

▼

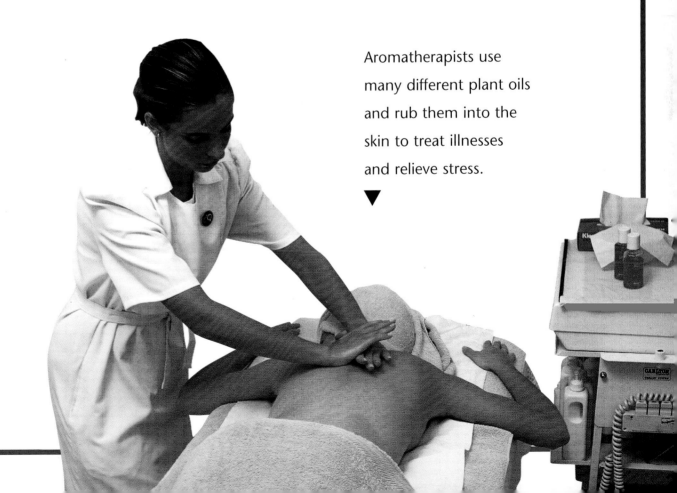

Animals' Senses of Smell

Some animals have a very sensitive sense of smell and can detect smells which are too weak for humans to detect. An animal's sense of smell can play an important part in helping it to stay alive.

▲

Some animals rely on their own smell for protection. When it senses danger, a skunk releases a foul-smelling chemical to keep other animals away.

Animals, such as deer, are hunted by other animals for food. A deer's sense of smell is so **acute** that it can pick up the scent of the hunter carried towards it by the wind. This gives the deer time to run away and so avoid being caught.

Animals can recognize each other by their smell. If a farmer wants a ewe to look after an **orphaned** lamb, he may rub this lamb against the ewe's own lamb. The orphan will then smell like her own lamb and the ewe will look after the baby as her own.

▲

Lambs may all look alike, but each has its own individual smell. A ewe knows her own lambs by their smell.

◄ Dogs can be trained to detect certain smells. A sniffer dog is being used by customs officers to search luggage for dangerous items such as drugs and explosives.

When Things Go Wrong

Our senses of taste and smell can be affected by many things. If our nose is blocked because of a cold or hayfever we often cannot smell properly. We probably cannot taste the flavour of our food very well either.

▲
An injury to the nose may reduce the sense of smell.

Injury to the nose from a fall or sports accident can affect the sense of smell. If the **nerves** that carry messages from the nose to the brain are damaged the sense of smell will be very much less, and in some cases may be destroyed completely.

Smoking cigarettes can damage the lining of the nasal cavity. The receptor cells in the lining of the nasal cavity cannot respond to chemicals as they usually do, so the sense of smell is reduced.

As people get older, their receptor cells are replaced less often so their senses of taste and smell gradually become less acute. This partly explains why babies and young children often prefer plain foods and why spicy foods taste much stronger to them than to adults.

This spicy food will taste a lot stronger to this young girl than to her grandmother. ▶

Glossary

acute A sharp sense of smell.

allergies Abnormal reactions of the body to things which are usually harmless.

artificial Made by man.

cartilage A strong material, rather like flexible bone.

cells Millions of tiny building blocks from which your body is made.

gravity The force which pulls everything towards the centre of the Earth.

nasal cavity The space at the back of the nostrils.

nerves Cells which carry signals to and from the brain.

orphan A child or animal without parents.

pore A tiny hole in a cell and in the surface of the skin.

salivary glands Organs in the mouth that produce saliva, a watery liquid which makes food easier to swallow.

virus A minute organism that can cause disease.

windpipe The tube which carries air to and from the lungs.

Books to Read

For younger readers

Smell (Senses series) by Mandy Suhr and Mike Gordon (Wayland, 1993).

Taste (Senses series) by Mandy Suhr and Mike Gordon (Wayland, 1993).

Eating and Tasting (Senses series) by Henry Pluckrose (Franklin Watts, 1997).

Sniffing and Smelling (Senses series) by Henry Pluckrose (Franklin Watts, 1997).

For older readers

Smell, Taste and Touch (Body Talk series) by Jenny Bryan (Wayland, 1993).

Index